KB244205

# The Secret of
# the Golden Ratio

Happy House

# About Wise & Wide

- A systematic 6-level English reading program based on Lexile® measures
- Diverse and interesting topics chosen from the elementary curriculums of Korea and English speaking western countries
- Well-written books in various forms including fiction stories, descriptive texts, and classics retold
- The informative but original fiction stories grab your interest, leading to the easy and clear understanding of the educational content.
- Improve thinking skills with solid after-reading activities at all levels of the series.

**Wise & Wide** is a 6-level English reading program that consists of 60 books and each level is systematically divided by Lexile® measures. The Lexile® Framework for Reading is the most popular reading measuring system in American formal education curriculums and many English programs. Over 20 out of 50 states in the U.S. mark Lexile® measures directly on students' final report cards and over 300 well-known publishers adopt and use Lexile® measures.

Experience many kinds of readings written by professional writers from the U.S. and England. They used interesting topics that were carefully chosen after analyzing elementary curriculums from around the world including Korea, the U.S., England, and Australia among many others. Comprehensive after-reading activities including graphic organizers, speaking tasks, and After-reading Tests are ready for you.

### Levels in the series and their corresponding Lexile® measures

| Level | Lexile® measures | U.S. Grade |
| --- | --- | --- |
| Level 1 | Below 200L | Pre K - K |
| Level 2 | 190L - 400L | Lower Grade 1 |
| Level 3 | 350L - 530L | Upper Grade 1 |
| Level 4 | 420L - 650L | Grade 2 |
| Level 5 | 520L - 940L | Grade 3 - 4 |
| Level 6 | 830L - 1070L | Grade 5 - 6 |

* Smart Readers: Wise & Wide level 1 is applicable to the preschool level in the U.S.

* The source of the relationship between Lexile® measures and U.S. school grades: CCSS(Common Core State Standards) FOR ENGLISH LANGUAGE ARTS, APPENDIX A (2012, which is used by 45 states in the U.S.)

# Topic List

| | Level 1 | Level 2 | Level 3 | Level 4 | Level 5 | Level 6 |
|---|---|---|---|---|---|---|
| Book 1 | Science>Biology: The hibernation of animals Story | Science>Biology: Living and nonliving things Story | Science>Biology> Animals & the Environment: Sea otters Story | Environment> Living with nature: The diver & the persimmon tree Story | Science>Biology> Animal: Amazing animals of the Amazon Story | Science>Biology: Germs, transmitted diseases Story |
| Book 2 | Literature> World classics: Aesop's fables Story | Literature> Traditional fairy tale: Old tales about stones Story | Social Studies> Economy: To run a business to make and save money Story | Science>Biology> Plants: Photosynthesis Story | Science>Earth science: Earth's layers, earthquakes, volcanoes, and earth's atmosphere Report | Mathematics> Sequence: The golden ratio & the Fibonacci sequence Story |
| Book 3 | Science>Physics: How shadows are formed Story | Literature> World classics: Peter Pan Story | Science>Scientific technology: Nanobots Story | Literature>Myths: World's creation stories Story | Literature> Legend: The story of King Arthur Story | Literature>Myths: Constellation myths Story |
| Book 4 | Literature> Traditional literature: The Talmud Story | Science>Biology> Animal: Polar bears Story | Science>Biology> Animal: Mountain gorillas Story | Social Studies> Cultural anthropology: Amazing ancient cultures of the world Story | Science> Earth science: Clouds and weather Story | |
| Book 5 | Social Studies> Ethics: Rules in   daily life Story | Science>Biology> The five senses Report | Social Studies> Cultural anthropology: Astonishing festivals Report | Art>Music: Stories from two operas Story | Social Studies> World culture & history: The Renaissancer Story | |
| Book 6 | Social Studies> World geography & travel: Tourist attractions around the world Story | Science>Biology> Animal: Dinosaurs Report | Science>Biology> Astronomy: The solar system Story | Social Studies> People: Three great people who overcame hardships Story | Science> Scientific technology: The wonderful world of robots Report | |
| Book 7 | | | | Science & Social Studies> Technology & culture: Inventions from around the world Report | Art> Works of art: Famous paintings Report | |
| Book 8 | | | | | | |
| Book 9 | | | | | | |
| Book 10 | | | | | | |

* 10 books in each level will be published.

# How to Use This Book

## • Before Reading

You can easily find the topic and what kind of story you are about to read.

## • The text

All the stories were written by professional writers from the U.S. and England, so you will read authentic and appropriate English sentences and expressions in every book in the series.

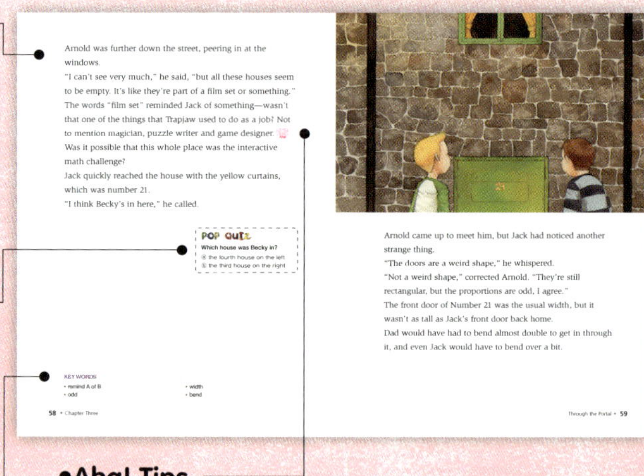

## • Pop Quiz

Check out right away if you understand what you have just read by solving a pop quiz that checks your comprehension.

## • Key Words

The key words and expressions on each page are listed for you to easily study them.

## • Aha! Tips

Download free Korean explanations at *www.ihappyhouse.co.kr* for all of the sentences marked with "Aha!". These explain cultural, scientific, and economic knowledge or they deal with aspects of English such as grammatical structures or idiomatic expressions. There are lots of "Aha! Tips" to help you understand the text.

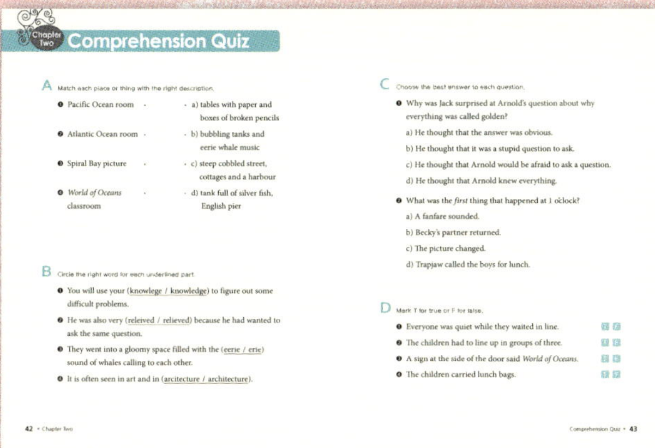

### •Comprehension Quiz

After reading one chapter, solve various questions to find out if you fully understand the content.

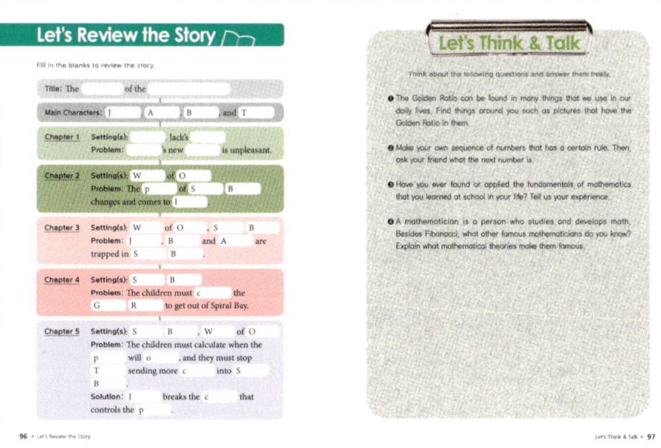

### •Let's Review the Story /
### •Let's Think & Talk

Fill in the blanks in the organizer to summarize the whole story. Express your own thinking and feelings about the story by answering the questions. You can build up logic and reasoning skills for your essay examinations in the future.

## Appendix

### Audio CD

In the CD audio book form, the texts are read vividly by American professional voice actors.

### After-reading Test

Solve an additionally provided After-reading Test for each book.

### The Korean translation, Answer Keys, a Word Quiz, a Word List, and Aha! Tips for each book

You can download them for free at *www.ihappyhouse.co.kr*

# Before Reading

## The Secret of the Golden Ratio

Level 6-2, Lexile® 840L | •Mathematics〉Sequence •Story

### The "Golden Ratio" hidden in nature

Does your head start to ache when you think of "math"? Well, you might change your mind completely after you read the book. If you think math is a difficult subject full of complicated calculations and incomprehensible formulas, you have misunderstood its usefulness. Math is a mysterious key that helps us understand the world that we live in.

Do you know the fact that things or pictures that we feel are beautiful are this way because they follow a certain mathematical ratio? The ratio is even hidden in nature such as in plants and animals. It was the mathematician Fibonacci who found out this amazing secret.

We invite you to an exciting adventure about the sequence of numbers and the Golden Ratio that he discovered!

## Summary

The first meeting between Mr. Tapshaw, who came to teach the class instead of the sick homeroom teacher, and our main character Jack didn't go well. Jack didn't concentrate on the class and was scolded again and again. Mr. Tapshaw explained the Fibonacci sequence and the Golden Ratio with zeal, but Jack who hated math didn't listen to the explanation well and had soccer on his brain. He didn't realize it at that time, but he was making a big mistake. The explanation that he missed was a crucial clue for the "interactive math challenge" that he would take part in later.

Led by Mr. Tapshaw, Jack went on a field trip to "World of Oceans" with his classmates, including Becky his twin sister, and Arnold, to take part in the "interactive math challenge". While at "World of Oceans, the three of them got trapped when they went into a miniature village. To open the firmly closed door, they have to solve a math puzzle and enter the answer which is the password, at one of several specific times. Will they be able to solve the math puzzle to escape?

# Contents

# The Secret of the Golden Ratio

# The Secret of
# the Golden Ratio

# Chapter One

# The Fibonacci Sequence

"Welcome to the class, children, and sit down quickly, please," said the new teacher.

Jack nudged his friend, Nathan, and muttered, "What's going on? Who's he, and what's he doing here?"

"He's a substitute teacher, I think," whispered Nathan, "but I've never seen him before."

"Good morning, class," said the teacher, in a deep voice. "My name is Mr. Tapshaw and I'll be here for the next week or two while your regular teacher, Miss Bradley, is ill. I have had many different jobs in my life, including: computer game designer, maker of film sets, puzzle writer, part-time magician, and recently I've become a teacher."

"I wonder what's wrong with Miss Bradley?" whispered Jack to Nathan.

**KEY WORDS**

- nudge
- mutter
- substitute
- whisper
- set
- part-time (↔ full-time)
- regular
- in a deep voice
- slam down
- boom

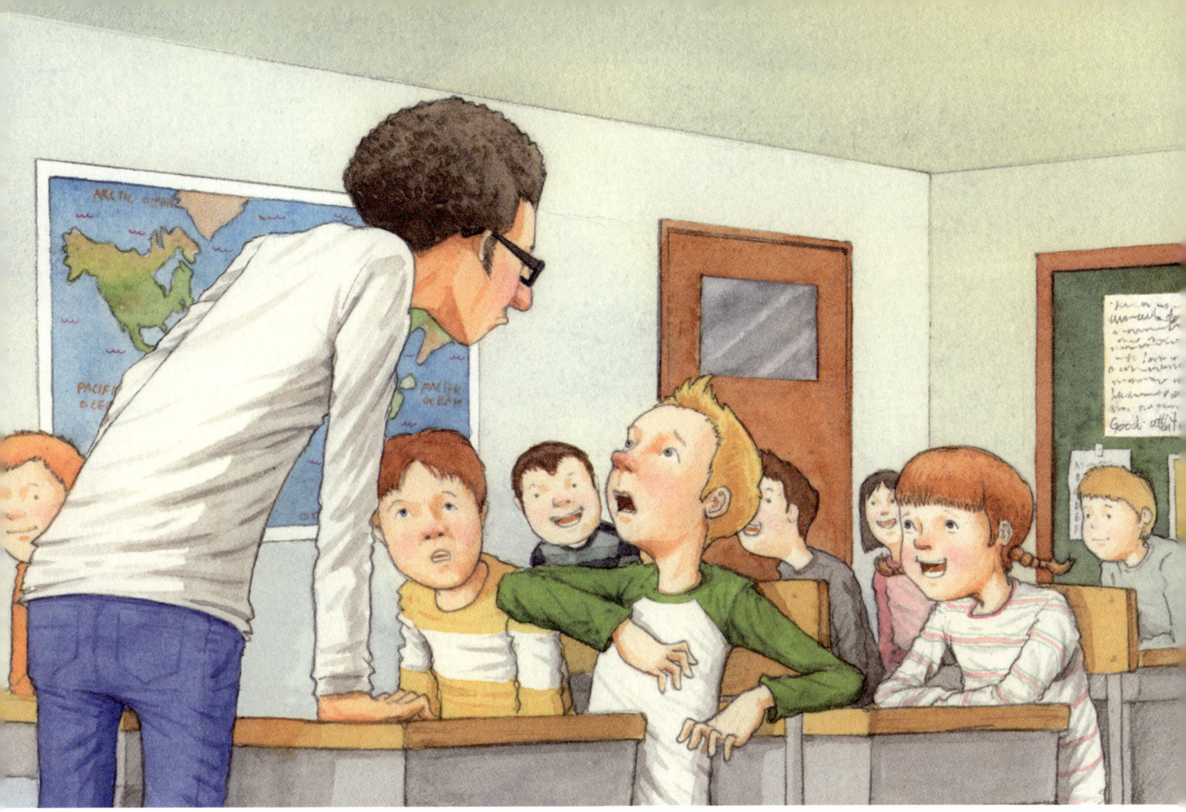

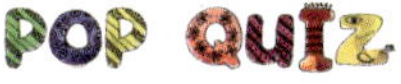

A hand slammed down on the desk in front of them and the new teacher boomed, “Are you listening to me? What’s my name?”

Jack thought hard, but he just couldn’t remember what the man had said his name was.

**POP QUIZ**

**Where does the opening paragraph take place?**

ⓐ in a school

ⓑ in a house

He glanced at Nathan and raised his eyebrows in a silent plea for help.

*Tap-shaw*, mouthed Nathan, exaggerating the movements of his mouth.

"Er... is it Trapjaw?" stammered Jack.

The entire class exploded into laughter, and Mr. Tapshaw turned a shade of crimson.

His eyes glittered behind his rectangular glasses, and he glared at Jack for a few moments before turning away.

Perhaps if Jack hadn't accidentally upset him that first day, the rest might never have happened; or maybe Trapjaw had planned it all along.

## POP QUIZ

**Why did Mr. Tapshaw get angry with Jack?**

ⓐ Because he didn't listen to Mr. Trapshaw.
ⓑ Because he didn't study hard.

**KEY WORDS**

- glance at
- plea
- mouth
- exaggerate
- Trapjaw
- stammer
- explode into laughter

- shade
- crimson
- glitter
- rectangular
- glare at
- turn away
- accidentally

- upset
- the rest
- announce
- groan
- multiplication table
- ancient

"Today," he announced, "we are going to study mathematics."

Jack groaned to himself because if there was one thing he hated, it was math.

Some people seemed to find it so easy to remember their multiplication tables, but not him.

"Math, my friends, is the key to the universe!" said Trapjaw.

He went to the front of the room and pointed at a picture of some ancient Italian man.

"This is Fibonacci, who is known as the father of mathematics."

Across the room, Arnold Blenkinsop raised his hand and said, "I know something about Fibonacci!"

Trapjaw smiled, showing even rows of rectangular teeth. "Would you like to tell the rest of the class?"

**KEY WORDS**

- even
- row
- prefer A to B
- subject
- mathematician
- the Middle Ages
- sequence
- drift into
- daydream
- involve
- fame

Arnold preferred books to people, and he seemed to know something about every subject in the world, so nobody was surprised when he announced, "Fibonacci was born in the town of Pisa, Italy, in the twelfth century.  Some people call him the greatest European mathematician of the Middle Ages."

"Correct," said Trapjaw, "but does anyone else know why he is famous?"

Nobody raised their hand, so Arnold began to explain about something called the Fibonacci Sequence, while Jack drifted into a daydream involving soccer and fame.

**POP QUIZ**

**What country did Fibonacci come from?**

ⓐ Spain
ⓑ Italy

"You, boy!" snapped Trapjaw. "Are you falling asleep during my lesson?"

Jack sat up when he saw that Trapjaw was glaring right at him, his mouth fixed in a straight line.

"I have written the Fibonacci sequence on the board," he said, "and I would like you to tell me what is the next number in the sequence."

Jack looked at the board, which had a series of numbers written on it:

1, 1, 2, 3, 5, 8, 13...

Jack looked quickly at Nathan for help, but Nathan just shrugged his shoulders.

"Er... is it fourteen?" said Jack, cautiously.

"Now, why would it be fourteen?" said Trapjaw. "How does that fit the pattern?"

**KEY WORDS**

- snap
- sit up
- straight line
- a series of
- shrug one's shoulders

- cautiously
- fit
- pattern
- closely

"Was there a pattern?" thought Jack, thinking that perhaps he should have listened a little more closely. The first two numbers were the same, and then it was 2 and 3, but why did it suddenly jump to 5, and then 8?

Arnold raised his hand again.

"It's twenty-one!" he said, wriggling about in his seat as though he was trying to polish it with his butt. 

"That is correct, but why is it twenty-one?" asked Trapjaw.

Jack leaned in close to listen properly this time.

"You just add together the last two numbers each time," said Arnold, "and that gives you the next one."

"Would you come out to the front and write it down?" said Trapjaw.

Arnold nodded eagerly and jumped out of his seat. His hand was steady as he wrote on the board:

$1 + 1 = 2$

$1 + 2 = 3$

$2 + 3 = 5$

$3 + 5 = 8$

$5 + 8 = 13$

$8 + 13 = 21$

$13 + 21 = 34$

**POP QUIZ**

What would be the next two numbers in this Fibonacci sequence?

1, 1, 2, 3, 5, 8, 13, 21, ______, ______

**KEY WORDS**

- wriggle about
- as though
- polish
- butt
- lean in close
- eagerly
- steady

1, 1, 2, 3, 5, 8, 13...
1 + 1 = 2
1 + 2 = 3
2 + 3 = 5
3 + 5 = 8
5 + 8 = 13
8 + 13 = 21
13 + 21 = 34

Jack watched a stray drop of rain splatter against the window, and thought that it was going to be a very long morning.

When they had written down the first twenty numbers of the Fibonacci sequence, Trapjaw showed them some more pictures.

There were pictures of spirals, buildings, and famous paintings, which were all supposed to be especially beautiful for people to look at.

▲ a spiral

Trapjaw began to explain about something called the Golden Ratio, but Jack stopped listening, his brain exhausted. He didn't know what the Golden Ratio was, and he didn't care. After all, he wouldn't ever need it for anything important, would he?

# [The Golden Ratio in our daily lives]

▲ TV screen

▲ the Parthenon

▲ the building of the UN General Assembly

▲ a spiral galaxy

When he got home, Mom was in the kitchen, baking cookies.
"Is that you, Jack?" she called. "Is Becky with you?"
"She stayed behind after school to go to her dance club,"
said Jack.

He didn't want to walk home with his sister, Becky, since she
was always teasing him and flicking her thin, ginger braids
in his face.

It was bad enough having to live with her, but because they
were twins, he even had to share the same class with her.

"What's this?" said Mom, pulling a letter out of Jack's school bag. "You're going on a field trip—how exciting!"

"Mom, we're only going to *World of Oceans*," groaned Jack, "and I've been there five million times already."

"But it says there's going to be an interactive math challenge, which might go on into the evening."

"A math challenge that goes on into the evening? That's even worse, Mom. Can't I be ill that day?"

Mom smiled, but she had already taken out a pen and was signing the bottom of the letter.

"Your teacher now has my permission," she said, "to make you do whatever math challenge he wants."

**KEY WORDS**

- stay behind
- tease
- flick
- ginger
- braid
- share
- field trip
- interactive
- challenge
- go on
- worse
- permission

**A** Mark T for true or F for false.

❶ Fibonacci is still alive today.  T  F

❷ Fibonacci lived in Europe.  T  F

❸ Fibonacci was born in Pisa.  T  F

❹ Fibonacci dreamed of football and fame.  T  F

**B** Circle the right word for each underlined part.

❶ Jack looked quickly at Nathan for help, but Nathan just (broke / shrugged / drew) his (shoulders / hands / pictures).

❷ Arnold's (head / face / hand) was steady as he (thought / pinched / wrote) on the board.

❸ Jack didn't want to (walk / dance / leave) home with his (aunt / brother / sister), Becky.

❹ Because they were (friends / rival / twins), they even had to share the same (bedroom / class / detention) with each other.

  Choose the best answer to each question.

❶ Why was Trapjaw teaching Jack's class?

a) He always taught math to them.

b) He was Jack's homeroom teacher.

c) He was taking the place of a teacher who was ill.

d) He was the school principal.

❷ Why was Arnold wriggling about in his seat?

a) He wanted to polish it with his butt.

b) He had an itch that he wanted to scratch.

c) He wanted to get up and play football.

d) He was eager to answer the question.

**D**  Fill in each blank with the right word below.

| slammed | glared | nudged | glittered |
|---|---|---|---|

❶ Jack ______________ his friend, Nathan.

❷ A hand ______________ down on the desk.

❸ Trapjaw's eyes ______________ behind his glasses.

❹ Trapjaw ______________ at Jack for a few moments.

# Chapter Two

# Golden Rectangles and Spirals

It was Monday, and Miss Bradley was still ill, so Trapjaw organized all the children into pairs for the field trip.

"Jack Smart?" he said, reading the list on his clipboard. "Your partner will be... Arnold Blenkinsop!"

Arnold grinned so widely that his little piggy eyes almost disappeared behind his plump cheeks.

He stood close to Jack and began to explain some weird facts about whales.

**POP QUIZ**

**Why didn't Miss Bradley lead the field trip?**

ⓐ She wasn't a math expert.
ⓑ She was absent due to illness.

**KEY WORDS**

- organize
- clipboard
- grin
- plump

- weird
- spoil
- recess
- precisely

- curve
- be good at
- fall on one's butt
- shriek

He wasn't a bad kid, but nobody really liked him because
he spoiled everybody's games at recess by telling them how
they could do things better.

"If you kick the soccer ball at precisely this angle," he would
say, "then it will curve round into the net."

"Show us!" Nathan would shout, but Arnold was no good at
soccer, and when he tried to kick the ball, he always fell on
his butt while everyone shrieked with laughter and pointed
at him.

Trapjaw made the children line up in pairs outside the glass-
fronted building, which was painted with tropical fish.

*World of Oceans* said the sign above the doorway.

Trapjaw walked up and down the line, and nobody dared to
whisper or rustle their lunch bag.

"Don't forget that this is a math excursion," he said, looking
directly at Jack. "You will use your knowledge to figure out
some difficult problems."

First of all, Trapjaw led them all into a classroom that was filled with tables and chairs.

On each table were some paper and a box full of pencils, most of them broken or blunt.

"Today we are going to discover what the Golden Ratio is," he said, "but first, we are going to find out about Golden Rectangles and Golden Spirals."

Arnold raised his hand and asked, "Why is everything golden?"

Jack blinked in surprise that there was something that Arnold didn't know after all!

He was also very relieved because he had wanted to ask the same question.

**What was painted on the building of *World of Oceans*?**

ⓐ the world
ⓑ tropical fish

**KEY WORDS**

- glass-fronted
- tropical
- doorway
- dare to
- rustle
- excursion
- figure out (= solve)
- first of all
- be filled with
- blunt
- discover
- blink
- relieved

"They are called *golden* because they are special, unique and beautiful," said Trapjaw.

"A golden rectangle has certain measurements that are very pleasing to look at. It is often seen in art and in architecture, and we can see one in the  famous painting, *Mona Lisa,* by Leonardo da Vinci."

He held up a picture of the painting.

"The measurements for a golden rectangle are taken from the Fibonacci sequence. Jack Smart, do you remember the first few numbers of the sequence?"

Jack gulped and tried to think. It started with 1, 2, 3... or did it? No, there was another 1 at the beginning, and then...

He shook his head, defeated.

"1, 1, 2, 3, 5, 8, 13!" shouted Arnold.

"That is correct," said Trapjaw, "and you will use these measurements to draw some golden rectangles.

**KEY WORDS**

- measurement
- pleasing
- architecture
- hold up

- gulp
- defeated
- long
- wide

- and so on
- as long as

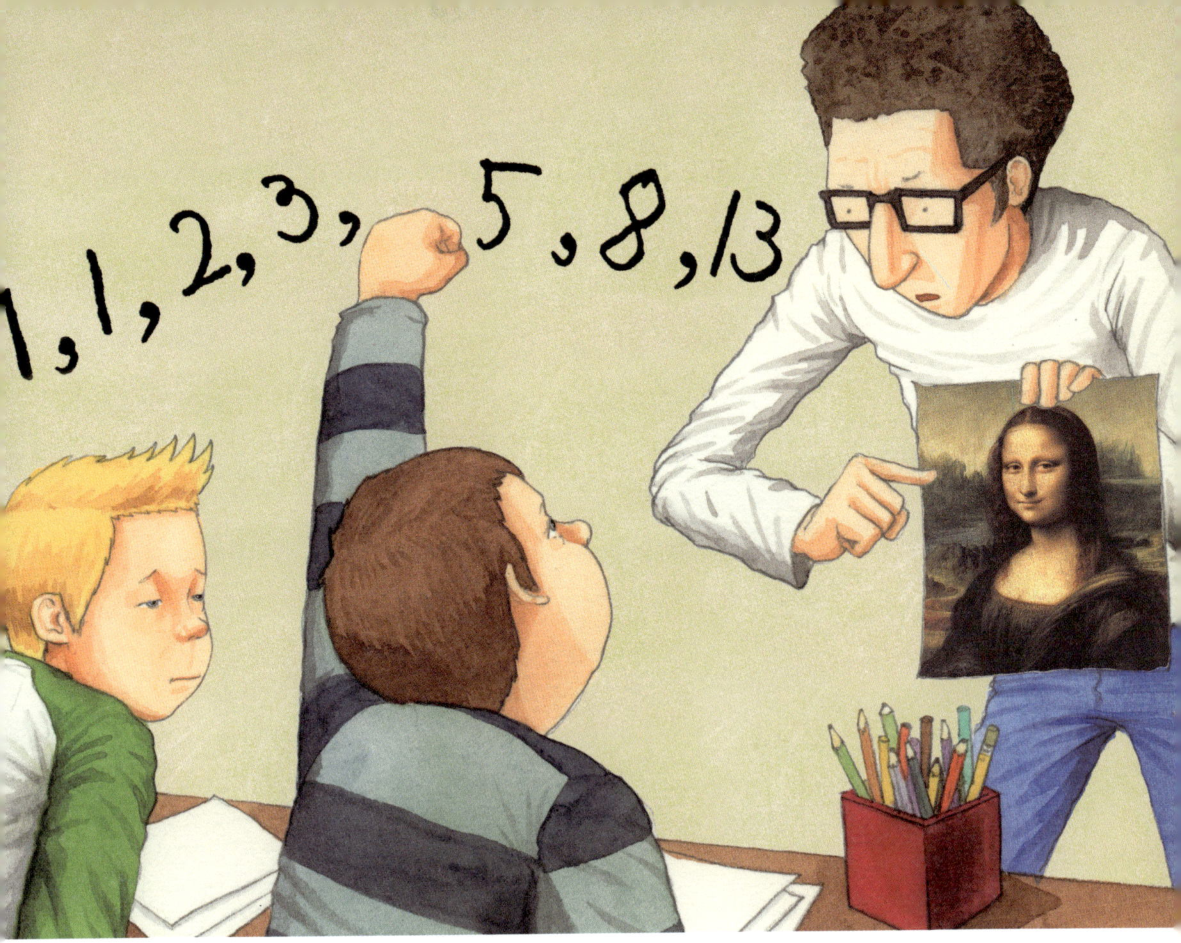


You can draw one that is 5 cm long and 3 cm wide, or you can draw one that is 8 cm long and 5 cm wide, and so on. Aha!
As long as you choose two numbers that are next to each other in the Fibonacci sequence, you will have a golden rectangle!"

**POP QUIZ**

**Who painted the *Mona Lisa*?**

ⓐ Fibonacci ⓑ Leonardo da Vinci

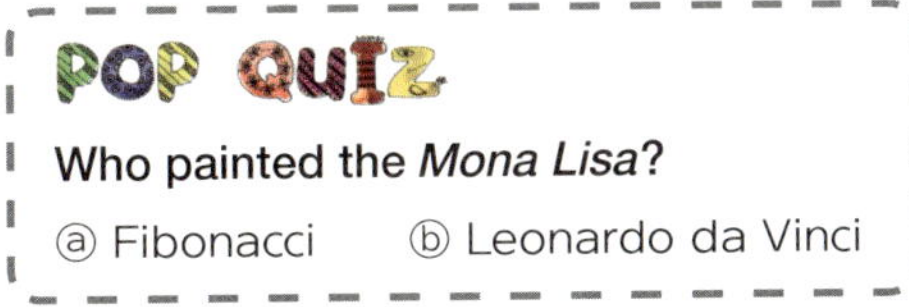

Ten minutes later, Jack had drawn some golden rectangles on his paper:

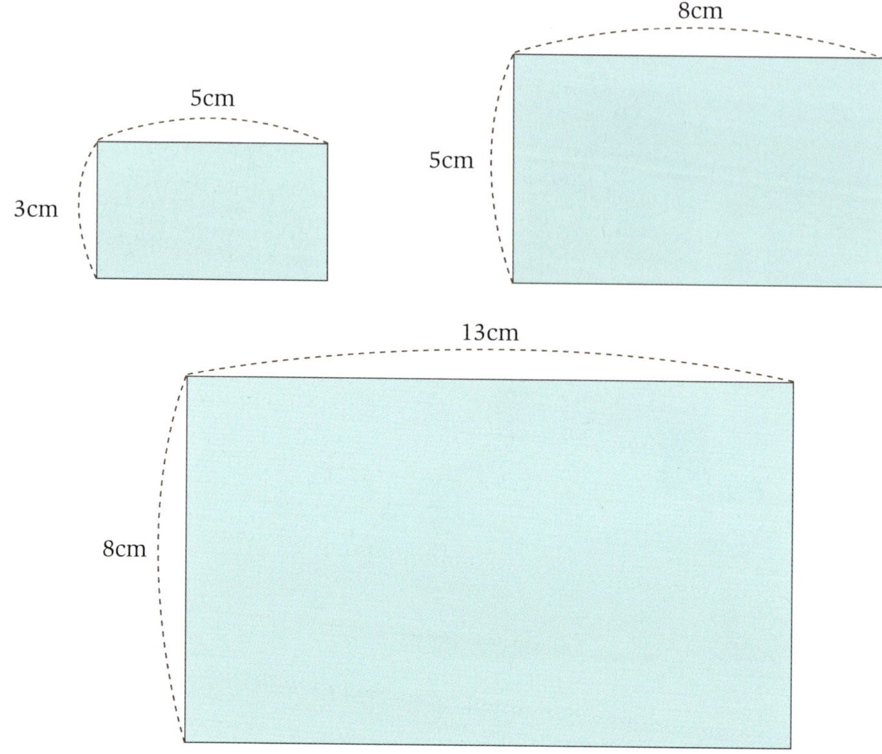


Trapjaw looked at his watch and said, "There is half an hour until lunchtime, so you can discover the next part yourselves. Your task is to find out what a Golden Spiral is. We'll meet in the lunchroom at 1 p.m. and you can share your findings."

**KEY WORDS**

- task
- lunchroom
- finding
- grab

- sticky
- march
- archway
- trot (= hurry)

- gloomy
- bubbling
- tank
- eerie

"Come on, Jack. Isn't this exciting?" said Arnold, and he
actually grabbed Jack's hand with his plump, sticky one.
Jack pulled it free and marched towards a nearby archway,
Arnold trotting after him.

They went beneath the archway into a gloomy space filled
with bubbling tanks and the eerie sound of whales calling to
each other.

## POP QUIZ

What time were the pupils told to meet for lunch?

ⓐ 1 p.m.

ⓑ 2 p.m.

"*Welcome to the Pacific Ocean*!" boomed a recorded voice as they entered.

Jack was astonished by all the amazing fish in the tanks and he pressed his nose against the glass, steaming it up with his breath.

"Look at this spiral," said Arnold, tapping at the glass of a cabinet packed with shells. "Perhaps it will help us with our task."

Jack peered at a perfect spiral shell that had been split in half to show the inside. It was separated into smooth, pearly chambers, each slightly larger than the next.

▲ a cross section of a nautilus

"It's called a nautilus," said Arnold, "and each chamber is bigger than the next by exactly the same proportion. How does a shellfish know how to do that?"

Jack was feeling confused again. As he glanced around the room, he noticed a small table in the corner.

"Hey, look over here, it shows you how to draw a golden spiral!"

Jack led Arnold to the table. They sat down on a tiny pair of chairs.

There was a card explaining how to draw a perfect spiral shell.

Arnold picked it up and Jack reached for a piece of paper, a pencil and a ruler.

"Okay," he said, "read the instructions to me."

Arnold cleared his throat. "The first thing you have to do," he said, "is to start with a golden rectangle."

Jack drew a rectangle, just as he'd done earlier. He chose to draw one that was 21 cm long and 13 cm wide.

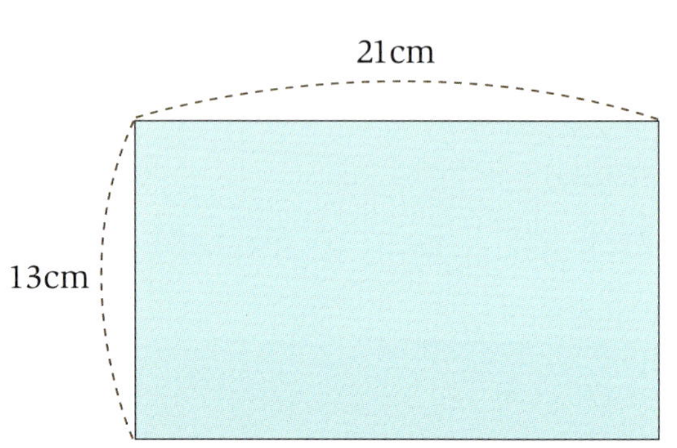


He was proud that he had remembered the numbers from the Fibonacci sequence.

By carefully following Arnold's instructions, Jack drew straight lines to divide the rectangle into squares.

He wrote the length inside each square.

"Look at that," he said.

"The numbers are all from the Fibonacci sequence."

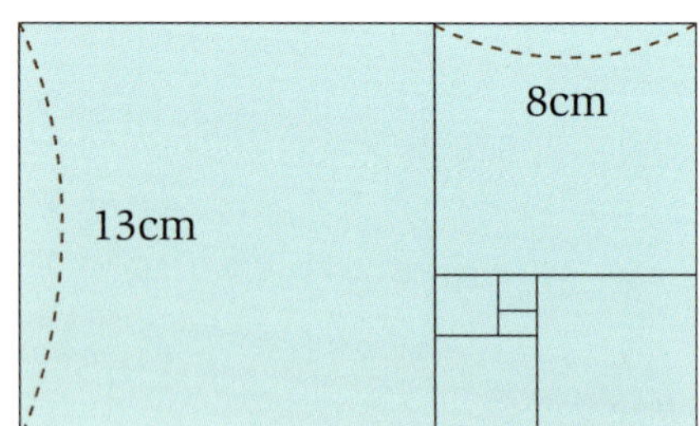

Now came the exciting part. All Jack had to do was to draw smooth curves from one corner to the next, and there it was—a perfect golden spiral.

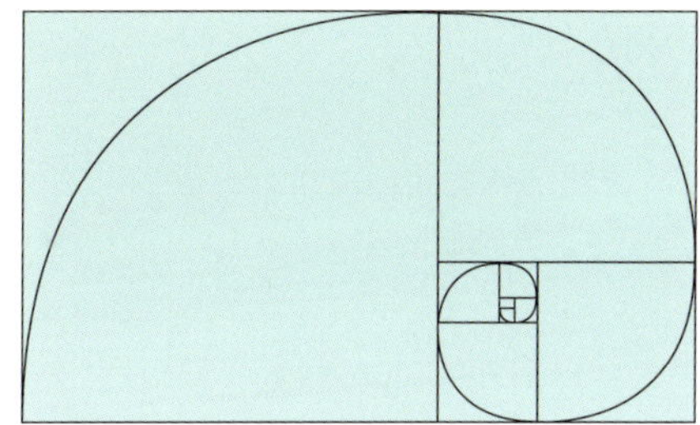

"You have to admit, that's a pretty cool way of using math," said Arnold, tracing the spiral with his finger.

"I suppose it would go on and on to infinity if you could draw it big enough."

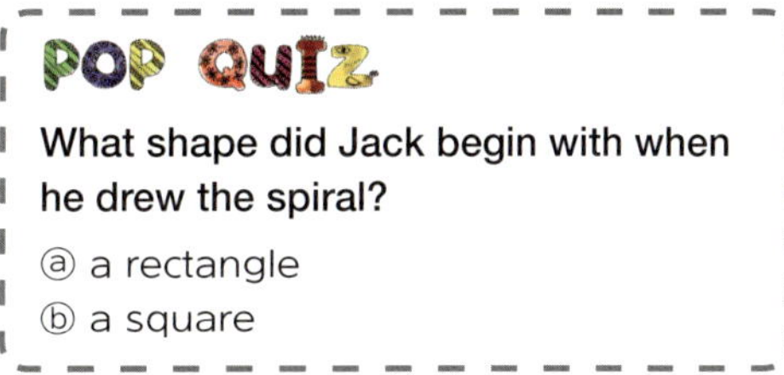


**KEY WORDS**

- pick ... up
- reach for
- instruction
- clear one's throat
- **draw** (draw-drew-drawn)
- divide
- square

- length
- corner
- admit
- trace
- suppose
- infinity

There was a sudden blast of music from the next room.

"I'm going to see what that is," Jack announced, getting up from his chair. He didn't really want Arnold to come, but Arnold stuck to him like gum on the bottom of his shoe. "*Welcome to the Atlantic Ocean*," boomed the same voice as they passed through the next archway.

This room was divided into different sections, and there was a tank filled with silver fish, gazing at nothing as they swam round in circles.

"You'd look better as fish and chips," Jack told them, tapping on the glass.

▲ fish and chips



- blast
- **stick to** (stick-stuck-stuck)
- **the Atlantic Ocean**

- section
- gaze at
- **swim** (swim-swam-swum)

In the corner was an area that looked like a harbour, with steps up to a pretend pier.

"*Welcome to the English Seaside,*" thundered the voice.

At the far end of the pier was a three-dimensional picture of a fishing village.

It must have been made of plastic, with the picture painted on, but it looked incredibly real.

**KEY WORDS**

- harbour
- step
- pretend

- pier
- thunder
- three-dimensional

- be made of
- incredibly

KEY WORDS
cottage
steep
cobbled
wind (wind-wound-wound)
tie up
fake
stick out
in case
stick to the rules
in a minute
hand
click
fanfare
unbelievable
drain

Two rows of stone cottages lined a steep cobbled street,
which wound down the hill toward a harbour where brightly
colored fishing boats were tied up.

It almost looked as though you could step into it.

A fake road sign stood at the side of the picture, pointing
down towards the harbour.

*Spiral Bay*, were the words printed on it.

But someone else was staring at it, too—Becky, standing
alone, peering into the picture.

"Hey, has your partner left you already?" Jack said.

Becky stuck out her tongue. "She's gone for lunch already
because she's scared to be even one minute late in case
Trapjaw gives her some math to do."

"Is it that time already? We'd better go, too.
You know what he's like about sticking to the rules."

"I'm coming in a minute," snapped Becky. "I'm just looking
at this picture."

The minute hand of the clock gave a loud click as it reached
the number 12.

It was exactly 1 o'clock when a fanfare of trumpets sounded
and the first unbelievable thing happened.

Becky must have seen it at the same moment as Jack,
because all the colour drained out of her cheeks.

The picture of Spiral Bay had changed.

# Comprehension Quiz

 **A** Match each place or thing with the right description.

❶ Pacific Ocean room   •

  • a) tables with paper and boxes of broken pencils

❷ Atlantic Ocean room   •

  • b) bubbling tanks and eerie whale music

❸ Spiral Bay picture   •

  • c) steep cobbled street, cottages and a harbour

❹ *World of Oceans* classroom   •

  • d) tank full of silver fish, English pier

**B** Circle the right word for each underlined part.

❶ You will use your (knowlege / knowledge) to figure out some difficult problems.

❷ He was also very (releived / relieved) because he had wanted to ask the same question.

❸ They went into a gloomy space filled with the (eerie / erie) sound of whales calling to each other.

❹ It is often seen in art and in (arcitecture / architecture).

❶ Why was Jack surprised at Arnold's question about why everything was called golden?

a) He thought that the answer was obvious.

b) He thought that it was a stupid question to ask.

c) He thought that Arnold would be afraid to ask a question.

d) He thought that Arnold knew everything.

❷ What was the *first* thing that happened at 1 o'clock?

a) A fanfare sounded.

b) Becky's partner returned.

c) The picture changed.

d) Trapjaw called the boys for lunch.

D Mark T for true or F for false.

❶ Everyone was quiet while they waited in line.  T  F

❷ The children had to line up in groups of three.  T  F

❸ A sign at the side of the door said *World of Oceans*.  T  F

❹ The children carried lunch bags.  T  F

# Chapter Three

# Through the Portal

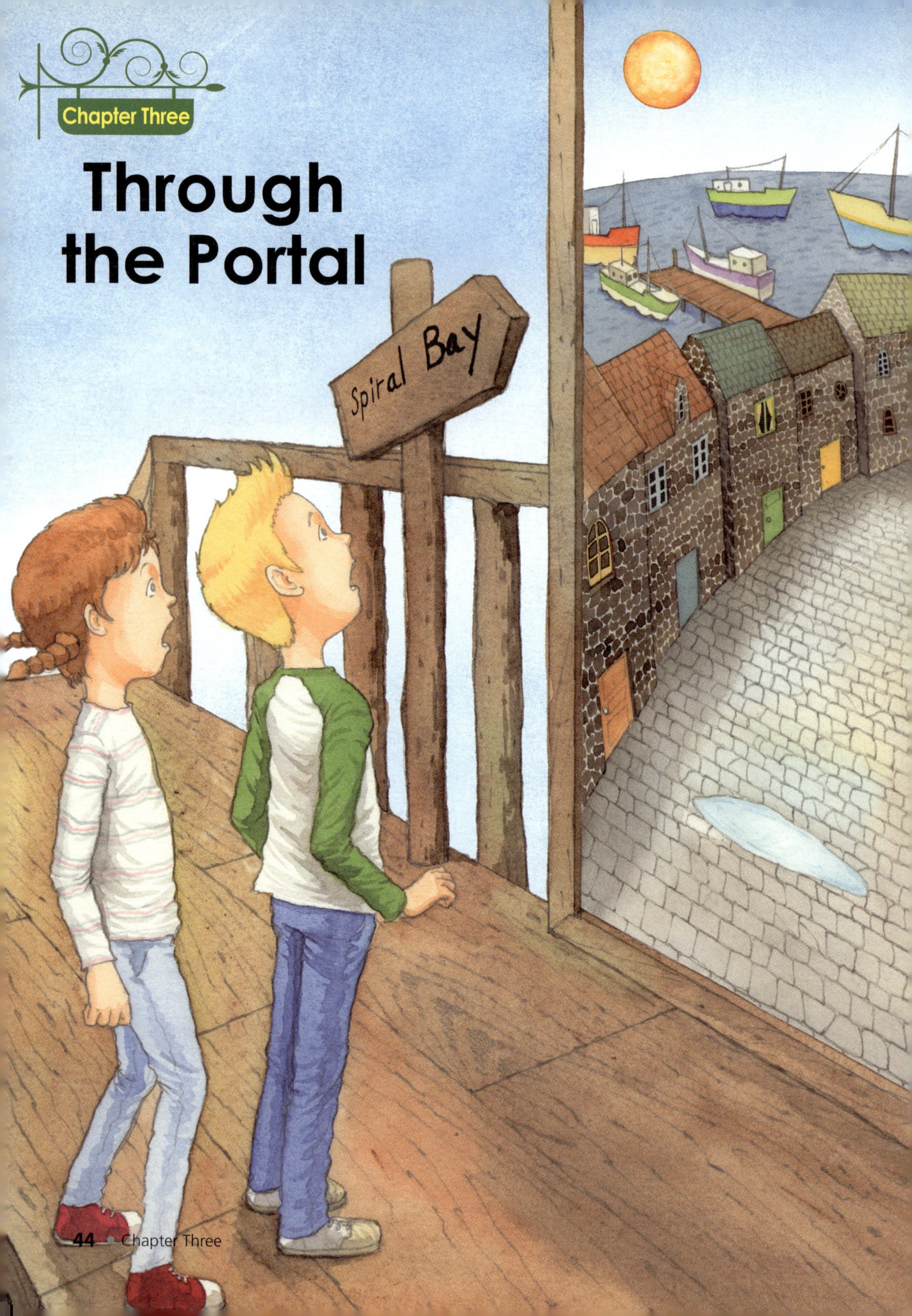

It was still the same picture, but somehow it looked more alive.

The stone of the houses was roughened, and the sun glittered on the puddles along the street.

Down in the harbour, the boats seemed to be moving on the waves, and a breeze lifted Jack's hair like a ghostly hand.

The clock hand clicked to one minute past the hour, and the breeze was gone.

The picture was flat, dull and lifeless once again.

"Did you see that?" asked Becky as she turned to Jack, eyes wide, but he didn't have time to answer her because Arnold was tugging at his arm.

"Come on, we'll be late, and then we'll get into trouble."

Reluctantly, Jack allowed himself to be dragged away from the picture and into the lunchroom.

Once they had eaten cheese sandwiches and drunk orange juice, Trapjaw asked each pair to explain what they had discovered.

Jack showed his drawing of the golden spiral, and everyone seemed impressed.

**KEY WORDS**

- **portal** (= entrance, gate)
- **somehow**
- **alive**
- **roughen**
- **puddle**

- **ghostly**
- **flat**
- **dull**
- **lifeless**
- **tug at**

- **get into trouble**
- **reluctantly**
- **allow oneself to**
- **drag**
- **impressed**

"The next challenge is to discover the value of the Golden Ratio," said Trapjaw. "This is where some of you may be involved in the interactive math challenge, so look out for it!"

The afternoon passed quickly.

Jack sketched a few fish, amazed by the varied colours and patterns, but he and Arnold didn't find any information about the Golden Ratio, or a math challenge.

At two o'clock, they passed the room with the Spiral Bay picture in it.

Jack heard the click of the minute hand, and the familiar trumpet fanfare.

He thought about going in to see if the picture would change again, but Becky was already staring at it with a frown on her face. He decided to avoid her this time.

So he went to look at the sharks instead.

**KEY WORDS**

- be involved in
- look out for
- amazed by
- varied

- frown
- gasp
- entrance
- **We'd better** (= We had better)

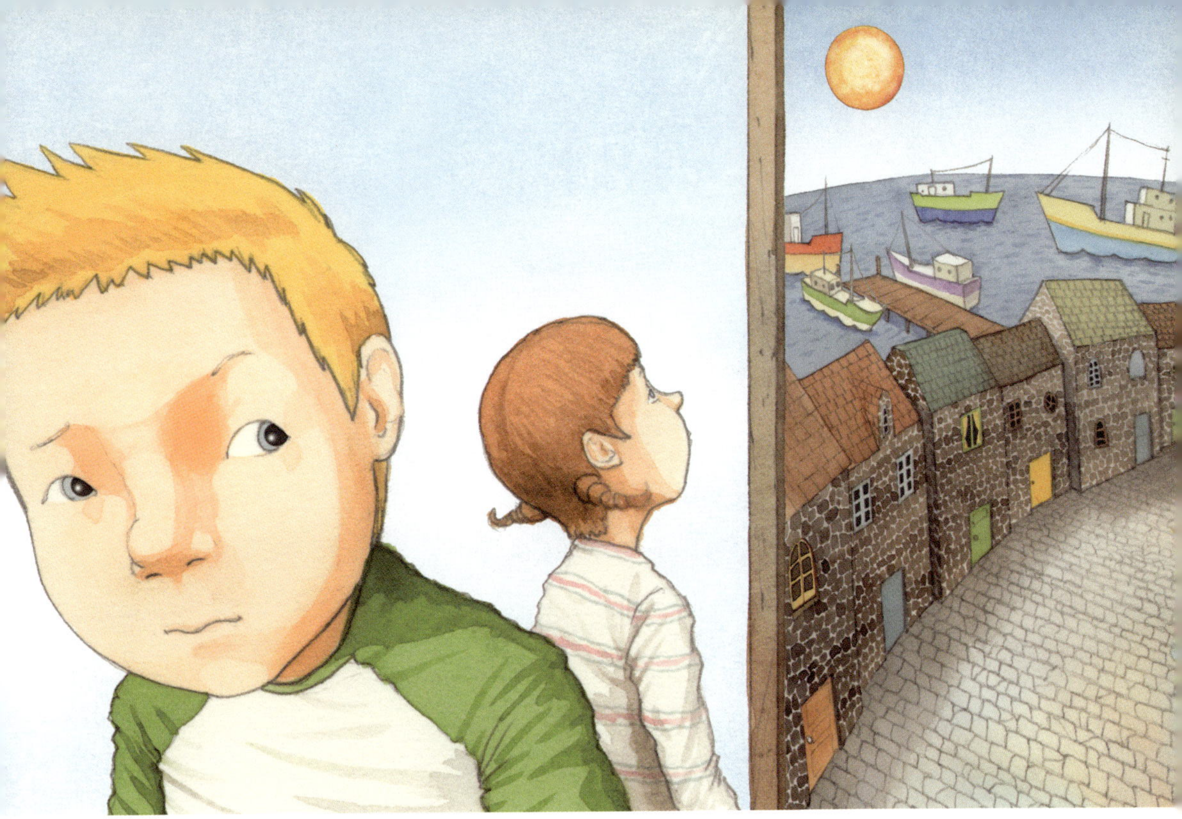

After a while, Arnold pulled out the cell phone his parents had bought him for getting 100% in his last math test.
He looked at the time, and gasped.
"Trapjaw said we had to be back at the entrance at 3:45, and it's 3:47. We'd better be quick!"

**POP QUIZ**

What did Jack draw?

ⓐ fish
ⓑ boats

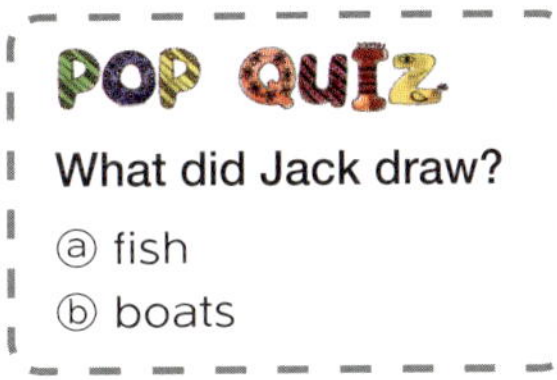

The other children were already getting onto the bus that
was waiting outside, in the rain.

Jack and Arnold joined the end of the line and Trapjaw
counted everyone.

"Only twenty nine," he shouted. "Who's missing?"

There was a rumble of voices. A girl said, "It's Becky. She
was my partner."

Jack raised his
hand and said,
"She was in the
Atlantic Ocean at
two o'clock."
The other children
giggled, but Trapjaw
didn't laugh.
"Then you'd better
go back and see if
she's still there," he
snapped. 

Jack nodded, and darted back
indoors.

As he passed through the first archway, the fish opened and
closed their mouths as though they were trying to tell him
something.

Under the second archway he hurried, back to the picture of
Spiral Bay.

He stepped up onto the fake
pier and stood in front of
the picture which, just as
before, was flat and silent.
But something was
different.
His heart began to pound,
and his hand trembled
as he pressed it against the
picture.

He couldn't believe what he was seeing, for in the upstairs
window of one of the cottages, a face
peered out.

It was a girl with thin, ginger plaits,
her hands pressed against the glass
and her mouth open as though
she was calling, or screaming.

"Becky!" he gasped.

Something caught
Jack's eye—something
that certainly hadn't
been there earlier in the
day.

A note was pinned to
the wall at the side of
the picture.

It said: *Can you solve the secret of Spiral Bay? The clock is ticking.*

Jack looked more closely at the writing, which looked familiar.

In fact, it looked exactly like the writing that covered the pages of his math book in red ink.

It was Trapjaw's handwriting.

**POP QUIZ**

Who was the first person to enter Spiral Bay?

ⓐ Becky

ⓑ Jack

**KEY WORDS**

- pound
- tremble
- peer out
- plait
- certainly
- pin
- tick
- writing
- handwriting

Suddenly, the hand of the clock clicked into place and the trumpets sounded to announce that it was four o'clock.

The picture came to life in an instant, and Jack stood there, the cool breeze sighing through his hair.

The sun gleamed off the puddles, making them look golden as Jack took a deep breath and stepped inside.

The first thing that struck him was how quiet it was. Aha!

There was no sound but the distant lap of water, the musical chink of the masts in the harbour and the faint sighing of wind around the chimney tops.

No seagulls, no cats, and no voices.

It felt as though there was nothing alive in this place except him, and that was a very spooky feeling indeed.

An invisible icy finger trailed down his spine and made him shudder.

## KEY WORDS

- come to life
- in an instant
- sigh
- gleam
- take a deep breath
- **strike** (strike-struck-struck)
- lap
- chink

- mast
- faint
- spooky
- indeed
- invisible
- trail
- spine
- shudder

POP QUIZ

Which of these did Jack hear in Spiral Bay?

ⓐ seagulls calling
ⓑ masts hitting each other

"Want some candy?" said a voice.

Jack whirled round and saw Arnold standing right behind him, holding out a paper bag and smiling hopefully.

"Arnold, how did you get in here?" he said.

Arnold shrugged and said, "The same way as you."

At first, Jack was annoyed that Arnold had followed him. But then, he was relieved that someone else was here with him, and also that it was someone smart.

"What is this place?" said Arnold as he pushed a piece of candy into his mouth and looked around.

"I don't know," replied Jack, "but I think that it must be some kind of huge room inside *World of Oceans*. It's got something to do with Trapjaw and his interactive math challenge. 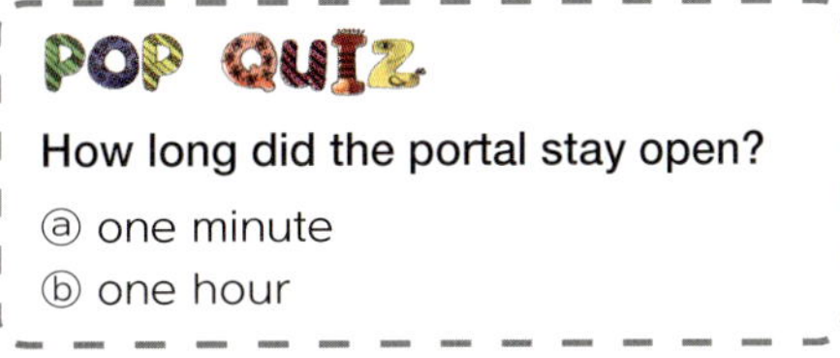 But Becky's in here too, so let's just find her and get out of here."

"Do you know that the portal thing…"—Arnold pointed at the doorway behind him —"is shut?"

It must have closed after one minute.



**KEY WORDS**

- whirl round
- hold out
- hopefully
- at first

- annoyed
- have got something to do with
  (have got = have)

Jack knew that the picture looked flat and ordinary from the other side, but here they were, trapped in this weird place.

"It's okay," he told himself, "because it'll open again in an hour, so all I need to do is find Becky and then we can get out of here."

He took a deep breath and stood with his back to the portal, looking down the street.

It curved away and down to the right like a giant nautilus shell.

Now, which was the house with the yellow curtains? There it was, a little way down, on the left hand side.

As Jack walked down the street, he noticed that the houses were numbered in a strange way.

Back home in his village, the streets all had the odd numbers on one side and the even ones on the other.

But the cottages here seemed to be numbered randomly.

The left hand side went 1, 3, 8, 21 and then he couldn't see any further.

The right hand side went 1, 2, 5 and then 13, which made no sense, although the numbers did seem oddly familiar.

**KEY WORDS**

- ordinary
- trap
- number

- odd number
- even
- randomly

- further
- make sense
- oddly

Arnold was further down the street, peering in at the windows.

"I can't see very much," he said, "but all these houses seem to be empty. It's like they're part of a film set or something."

The words "film set" reminded Jack of something—wasn't that one of the things that Trapjaw used to do as a job? Not to mention magician, puzzle writer and game designer. 

Was it possible that this whole place was the interactive math challenge?

Jack quickly reached the house with the yellow curtains, which was number 21.

"I think Becky's in here," he called.



**KEY WORDS**

- remind A of B
- odd

- width
- bend

Arnold came up to meet him, but Jack had noticed another strange thing.

"The doors are a weird shape," he whispered.

"Not a weird shape," corrected Arnold. "They're still rectangular, but the proportions are odd, I agree."

The front door of Number 21 was the usual width, but it wasn't as tall as Jack's front door back home.

Dad would have had to bend almost double to get in through it, and even Jack would have to bend over a bit.

Jack began to wonder whether this was all some kind of strange dream, and he half expected to wake up and find himself still in bed, in his pyjamas.

But this door was real enough, the green paint flaking beneath his knuckles.

"Becky?" he shouted, his voice echoing off the walls of the cottages opposite. "Becky, are you in there?"

Upstairs, a window opened and Becky's face appeared.

"Jack, is that you?" she said, almost sobbing. "I thought that nobody was coming, and I tried to get out of the painting, but I couldn't, and I thought I was stuck in the painting forever..."

Tears glistened on her cheeks as she dragged a hand across her face and sniffed.

Relief washed over Jack.

Now, all that they had to do was to wait until five o'clock, when the portal would open again, and all this would be over.

Becky came outside and argued with Arnold over the candy, and then the three of them wandered up to the portal to wait.

Jack watched the hands on his watch tick slowly round towards five o'clock. 4:58... 4:59... 5:00.

But there was complete silence—no fanfare, and no change in the flat surface of the portal.

In fact, nothing happened at all.

**KEY WORDS**

- expect
- flake
- knuckle
- echo
- sob
- glisten
- sniff
- relief
- wash over
- wander

 **A** Fill in each blank with the right word below.

| nodded | trembled | giggled | opened |
|---|---|---|---|

❶ The other children ______________, but Trapjaw didn't laugh.

❷ Jack ______________, and darted back indoors.

❸ The fish ______________ and closed their mouths.

❹ His hand ______________ as he pressed it against the picture.

**B** Mark T for true or F for false.

❶ Spiral Bay was part of a strange dream.    T  F

❷ All the odd-numbered houses were on one side of the street.    T  F

❸ The door of number 21 was painted green.    T  F

❹ Becky's face appeared at an upstairs window.    T  F

 Mark T for true or F for false.

① Why didn't Jack go in to look at the picture at 2 o'clock?

a) He didn't have time because he had to get to the bus.

b) He wasn't interested in the picture.

c) He was dragged away by Arnold.

d) He didn't want to talk to Becky.

② Why did Jack think that the portal would open at 5 o'clock?

a) He thought that it would open now that they had found Becky.

b) He thought that it opened every hour.

c) He thought that it was time to go home so they would be allowed to leave.

d) He thought that they had completed the math challenge.

**D** Put the sentences in order.

① Jack was relieved that Arnold was with him.

② Jack found Arnold offering him some candy.

③ Jack was annoyed that Arnold was with him.

④ Jack heard Arnold's voice.

________ → ________ → ________ → ________

# The Golden Number

"Why didn't it open?" wailed Becky.

"I'm going to call my parents," said Arnold, pulling out his cell phone.

But his face fell as the truth dawned. "There's no signal," he said, miserably.

"It must be something to do with the math challenge," said Jack. "We have to figure it out so that we can open the portal and get out of this place."

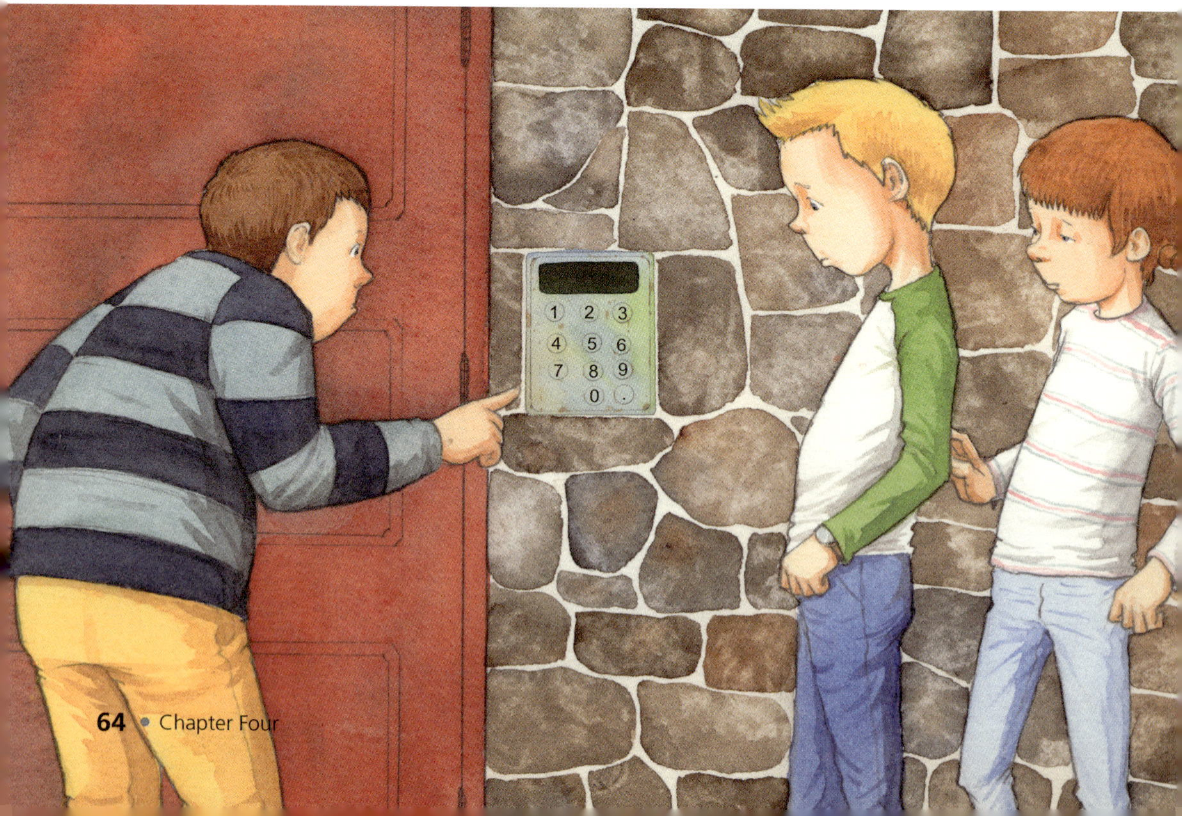

In the failing light, he noticed that there was a small keypad, like a calculator, set into the wall by the portal.

It had the numbers 0-9 on it, and also a decimal point. "There must be a code to get out!"

"What about the house numbers?" said Arnold as he looked down the street.

"They don't make any sense to me," groaned Becky.

"But if you take a number from one side of the street and then one from the other side, they make a pattern! 1, 1, 2, 3, 5, 8, 13, 21... Don't you recognize it?"

"It's the Fibonacci Sequence!" Jack had never been so glad in his life to remember something about math.

"That must be the code to get out."

Becky turned to the keypad and stabbed in the first three numbers, muttering, "One, one, two... What comes next?"

As she hesitated, a digital message flashed up on the keypad. *Input error*, it said; *six digits required.*

**KEY WORDS**

- wail
- fall
- dawn
- signal
- miserably
- failing

- keypad
- calculator
- decimal point
- code
- recognize
- stab

- flash up
- input
- digit
- require

"One, one, two, three, five, eight," said Jack, watching eagerly as Becky put the six digits in.

*Code incorrect; access denied*, said the blinking red message.

Becky sat down on the hard floor, her chin resting on her knees.

"What now, genius?" she said to Arnold.

Arnold shook his head and puffed out his cheeks. "It has to be something to do with the Fibonacci sequence, because this whole place is a huge golden spiral, and the doors are golden rectangles!"

Jack could see now that the doors looked like the rectangles he had drawn that morning, only bigger.

Everything about this place was one huge math puzzle, and it was all to do with that Fibonacci stuff.

"I'll try putting the number in backwards," suggested Becky, promptly keying in the number 853211.

*Access denied* came the message; *input golden number.*

"What does that mean?" said Becky and Jack at the same time, looking at Arnold for answers.

"It does sound familiar," he admitted. "I think that I might have read about it somewhere."

"Perhaps some of the house numbers are golden," said Becky.

Okay, it was a poor idea, thought Jack, but it was the only one they had.

"Arnold, you and Becky walk down that side of the street," he said, "and I'll go down this side."

"Why don't you and Becky go down one side and I'll go down the other?" said Arnold, anxiously.

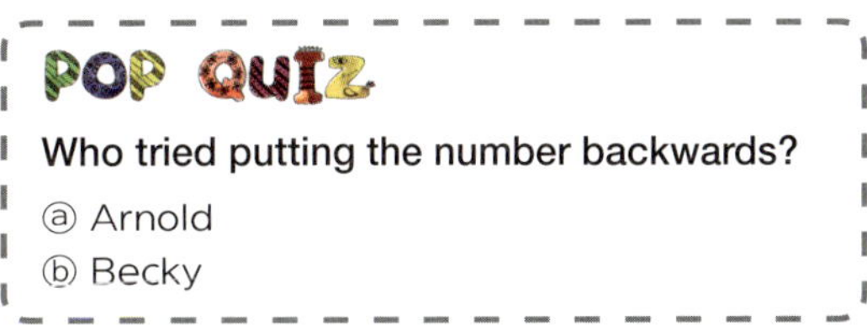


**KEY WORDS**

- incorrect
- access
- deny
- rest on
- puff out
- stuff
- backwards
- promptly
- key in
- anxiously

"I'd much rather go by myself!" shouted Becky, and she stamped off, hair swinging.

Arnold and Jack set off down the right hand side of the street, peering closely at the doors and hoping that one of the numbers might turn out to be made of gold—not real gold, of course, but brass, or whatever door numbers were made of.

They kept going, the street spiralling into a tighter curve. No wonder this place was called Spiral Bay!

It curled right round on itself and soon they passed beneath a sort of bridge with houses on it.

Jack realized that they were going in a circle and were actually passing underneath where they'd walked earlier.

It felt as though they were sliding down some kind of fairground ride, trapped inside a perfect golden spiral.

When they reached the end of the street, the houses ended and a sandy beach began.

**KEY WORDS**

| | | |
|---|---|---|
| • stamp | • tight | • fairground |
| • swing | • curl | • ride |
| • set off | • sort of | • sandy |
| • turn out | • underneath | |
| • brass | • slide down | |

Becky gave a shout, and pointed at the last house, where
a tiny note was pinned to the door, in the same neat
handwriting as before.

*The golden number is a ratio.*

Their task this afternoon was to find the Golden Ratio,
wasn't it?

Trapjaw had talked about it during that very first lesson, only
Jack hadn't been listening.

"Arnold," he said, urgently, "you must know what the
Golden Ratio is. You know everything!"

"I can't remember exactly," said Arnold.

"It's something to do with the Fibonacci sequence and the golden rectangles."

Becky frowned and said, "I can't remember what a ratio is."

Arnold blushed as he explained, "A ratio shows how one number relates to another. For example, the ratio of boys to girls here today is 2:1, which means that there are two boys to one girl."

"What does that have to do with anything?" said Becky, shaking her head.

"I need a pen and paper." Arnold looked at them hopefully. "Do you have any?"

Jack removed Trapjaw's note from the door and said, "You can use this, but I don't have a pencil."

"You could write in the sand with your finger," suggested Becky.

"I need a calculator, too," said Arnold.

"Use this," said Becky, taking Arnold's cell phone from his back pocket. "It has a calculator on it, doesn't it?"

**KEY WORDS**

- give a shout
- neat
- urgently
- blush
- relate to
- remove

Arnold smiled, rubbed his hands together and set to work, drawing in the sand with his forefinger.

"This could take a while," said Jack. "Becky, why don't we explore and see if there's another exit somewhere?" 

Becky said, "Perhaps there's a back door that opens with a regular lock and key, or we could even break it down."

And that's when Jack heard it—the fanfare of trumpets that announced the opening of the portal.



POP QUIZ

**Why didn't they run to the portal?**

ⓐ Because they didn't want to run.

ⓑ Because they couldn't make it in time.

**KEY WORDS**

- rub
- set to
- forefinger
- explore

- exit
- lock
- break down
- jerk up

- even if
- make sure

Becky's head jerked up too, and she cried, "We've missed it!"

The portal must have opened, but they were at the bottom of a steep and winding hill, and they would never make it back in time, even if they ran all the way.

"Six o'clock," said Jack, glancing at his watch. "Why didn't it open at five o'clock, when we were there, waiting to get out?"

"We'll keep looking for another way out," said Becky, "but let's make sure we're back up at the portal at 7 o'clock."

Jack's stomach began to rumble with hunger.

They were supposed to be home now. Surely people would be looking for them.

But the letter that Mom had signed said that the math challenge might go on into the evening, which meant that nobody would be worried yet.

Jack and Becky walked along the beach to the vertical cliffs at the far end, but there was no sign of any door, gate or magical portal.

Becky rested her palms against the smooth, cold rock and whispered, "What if we never get out of here?"

Suddenly, there was a cry behind them and they turned to see Arnold jumping up and down.

"I think I've found it!" he yelled. "I've figured out the Golden Ratio!"

## POP QUIZ

**Where did Jack and Becky go while Arnold was drawing in the sand?**

ⓐ to the portal
ⓑ to the cliffs

**KEY WORDS**

▪ vertical ▪ cliff ▪ palm

# Chapter Four · Comprehension Quiz

 **A** Match each word with its synonym.

❶ access

❷ denied

❸ incorrect

❹ remove

• a) wrong

• b) entry

• c) refused

• d) take out

**B** Choose the best answer to each question.

❶ Why were the doors unusually short?

a) Only children lived in Spiral Bay.

b) They had been badly made.

c) The houses were unusually small.

d) All the doors were Golden Rectangles.

❷ Why didn't the children run to the portal when it opened at six o'clock?

a) They didn't know that it had opened.

b) They were too far away to reach it in time.

c) They had given up on trying to escape.

d) They knew there was another exit somewhere else.

**C** Fill in each blank with the right word below.

| cold | neat | steep | magical |
|---|---|---|---|

❶ The portal must have opened, but they were at the bottom of a _______________ and winding hill.

❷ Becky rested her hands against the smooth, _______________ rock.

❸ A tiny note was pinned to the door, in the same _______________ handwriting as before.

❹ There was no sign of any door, gate or _______________ portal.

**D** Circle the right word for each underlined part.

❶ Becky sat down on the hard (spiral / floor / beach), her chin resting on her (knees / bag / face).

❷ They peered closely at the (floor / sea / doors) and hoped that one of the (children / numbers / notes) might turn out to be golden.

❸ Jack realized that they were going in a (square / rectangle / circle) and were actually passing (over / between / underneath) where they'd walked earlier.

# The Clock is Ticking

Arnold had written numbers all over the sand, some of them with several decimal places.

"Which one is it?" asked Jack.

"I think it's this one," said Arnold, pointing at a number that he'd circled: 1.6180

Becky looked at it doubtfully and said, "Shouldn't it have six digits if it's the code for the keypad?"

"There's a decimal point on the keypad," Jack pointed out, "so maybe that counts as one digit."

He didn't feel at all confident of Arnold's discovery.

"What kind of a weird number is that?" he said.

"I worked out the ratio between each pair of numbers in the Fibonacci sequence by dividing each number by the one before it," explained Arnold, pointing at the first calculation that he had scratched in the sand: $1 \div 1 = 1$

Arnold had laid everything out in a neat table, just like he always did in his math book at school, although this time the table was several meters long and wide.

| Fibonacci number | calculation | Ratio |
|---|---|---|
| 1 | | |
| 1 | 1 ÷ 1 = | 1 |
| 2 | 2 ÷ 1 = | 2 |
| 3 | 3 ÷ 2 = | 1.5 |
| 5 | 5 ÷ 3 = | 1.6666 |
| 8 | 8 ÷ 5 = | 1.6000 |
| 13 | 13 ÷ 8 = | 1.6250 |
| 21 | 21 ÷ 13 = | 1.6153 |
| 34 | 34 ÷ 21 = | 1.6190 |
| 55 | 55 ÷ 34 = | 1.6176 |
| 89 | 89 ÷ 55 = | 1.6182 |
| 144 | 144 ÷ 89 = | 1.6180 |
| 233 | 233 ÷ 144 = | 1.6180 |
| 377 | 377 ÷ 233 = | 1.6180 |
| 610 | 610 ÷ 377 = | 1.6180 |
| 987 | 987 ÷ 610 = | (1.6180) |

## POP QUIZ

How did Arnold calculate the Golden Ratio?

ⓐ by multiplying numbers
ⓑ by dividing numbers

**KEY WORDS**

- decimal place
- doubtfully
- point out
- count
- confident
- work out
- calculation
- scratch
- lay … out
- table

"Don't you see?" said Arnold, his face red with excitement.
"As you divide more and more numbers, they all come out to
the same answer every time."

Jack still wasn't sure, but it was the only idea they had, and
it was worth a try.

Becky linked her arm with Arnold's and they hurried away
up the hill.

Jack made his tired legs stride after them, one step after
another, past all the houses.

"Come on, Jack!" called Becky as she turned and waved to
him. "Let's do this all together!"

She seemed a lot more cheerful now, and Jack walked faster
to catch up.

"Think of supper!" yelled Arnold, his eyes glittering.

"Think of Mom's chocolate cake with orange frosting!"
laughed Becky.

**KEY WORDS**

- excitement
- come out
- worth
- link

- stride
- cheerful
- catch up
- frosting

- dreamily
- shore
- wash away

The three of them reached the portal together.

"You should put the number in, Arnold," said Becky, "since you discovered the golden thing."

"Golden Ratio," said Arnold, dreamily, as though he was talking about a new kind of donut.

Jack looked down the steep, cobbled hill toward the sea, where the waves were lapping gently at the shore, washing away Arnold's calculations.

"Quickly," he said. "You need to put the number in before you forget it!"

But Arnold was looking thoughtful and almost slightly sad.

"I suppose we could always come back…" he began.

"I never want to see this place again as long as I live," said Becky, "so just put in the number."

Arnold raised a trembling finger and tapped in the number: 16180.

"You put it in wrong!" said Becky. "You forgot the decimal point. Can you delete it?"

But there was no delete or backspace button on the keypad, only numbers and the decimal point.

A message flashed up, saying *Access denied; input golden number.*

"You do it, Jack," said Arnold, his voice wobbling.

"I'll tell you the number slowly and you put it in, while Becky watches to make sure it's right."

Jack nodded. He didn't dare to think what would happen if he got this wrong.

"One," said Arnold, "point… six… one… eight… zero."

Jack hardly dared to look when the message flashed up, saying *Access granted*.

Becky looked at Jack, her mouth open. "Does that mean...?"

They screamed, jumping up and down and hugging one another.

"We can go home! We can go home!" sobbed Becky.

Jack was the only one facing the portal.

He was the first one to notice that the picture was not changing and opening up.

The portal was still closed.

**POP QUIZ**

Who put the correct number into the keypad?

ⓐ Arnold

ⓑ Jack

Arnold sat down on the doorstep and banged his head against the portal.

"We must be able to work it out," he said, "if we just think about what we already know."

"We have to put in the golden ratio at the time when the portal opens," said Jack.

"The portal opens on the hour," said Becky, "but not every single hour."

"At first it opened every hour, but then it didn't after that," said Arnold, looking thoughtful as he pulled his cell phone from his pocket once more. "Jack, what time was it when you first noticed the portal was open?"

"Becky and I saw it together at one o'clock, when I was telling her to come for lunch."

"Then it was open again at two o'clock," said Becky, "and I came in at three o'clock."

"Arnold and I came in at four o'clock, but it was closed at five o'clock," said Jack, "and it opened again at six."

Arnold screwed up his face as though he were thinking.

"I need something to write with."

"Oh, please don't make us go back down to the beach," begged Becky.

Arnold found a tiny stub of pencil in his pocket and held out his hand for Trapjaw's note. It was hardly big enough to write on, but it would have to do.

Arnold turned the note over and began to draw another table. Arnold held up the paper and asked, "Do you notice anything?"

"It's those Fibonacci numbers again," growled Becky, "which I am beginning to hate."

**KEY WORDS**

- doorstep
- bang
- on the hour
- screw up one's face
- beg
- stub
- do
- turn … over
- growl

"They're showing a pattern, aren't they?" said Jack, "so we can work out the next time the portal will open."

"I hope so," muttered Arnold as he filled in more of the table:

| Time portal opened | Number of hours since first open |
| --- | --- |
| 1 pm | |
| 2 pm | 1 |
| 3 pm | 2 |
| 4 pm | 3 |
| 6 pm | 5 |
| 9 pm | 8 |

"If I'm correct, then the portal will next open exactly 8 hours after it first opened."

"That would be 9 p.m.!" gasped Becky. "Do you mean that we have to wait all that time before we can try again?"

"And if we miss it," said Arnold, nodding in agreement, "then the next time will be 13 hours after the initial opening, which would be…"

He screwed up his face as he worked it out in his head, then wrote something down on the note.

"2 o'clock in the morning."

The next couple of hours passed very slowly as the sky grew darker and the air grew colder.

Jack shivered, and wrapped his arms across his chest.

What would happen if they didn't get out of here at 9 o'clock? Surely Mom and Dad would start asking questions then?

They would want to know where he and Becky were.

As 9 o'clock approached, it was so dark that he could barely see the faces of the others.

8:45 p.m. ... 8:50... 8:55... 8:58...

"Get ready," Jack whispered. "Arnold, make sure you get the number exactly right this time."

They all stood up, breathing hard in the darkness around the portal.

Then, the fanfare sounded, and the message on the keypad flashed up: *input golden number*.

Arnold stabbed in the ratio he had calculated: 1.6180

*Access granted* said the glowing message.

**KEY WORDS**

- fill in
- in agreement
- initial

- shiver (= tremble)
- wrap
- barely

- breathe hard
- glow

There was a strange shimmering sensation, and suddenly Jack could see the room beyond the portal, inside *World of Oceans*. There were the aquarium tanks and the fish swimming lazily around in them.

"Go through quickly, before it closes!" he yelled, pushing Becky and Arnold as hard as he could.

The three of them fell through in a heap onto the floor of the room.

**KEY WORDS**

- shimmer
- sensation
- in a heap
- all at once
- squeal
- shrill

There was screaming all around, and for a moment Jack couldn't work out what had happened.

Had something gone wrong? Were Becky and Arnold injured? Then Becky's hands lifted him to his feet, patting him and hugging him all at once.

"We did it!" she squealed, her voice so shrill in his ear that it hurt. "We can go home!"

"Congratulations," said a voice from the shadows.

Trapjaw stepped forward, a smile on his face.

"Don't worry; if you hadn't got out, I would have come in to help you. I wouldn't have let you stay in there all night, although I would have liked to see how you managed in there without Arnold. Next time, I must be careful to make sure I control things better."

"Next time?" spluttered Jack, hardly able to believe his ears. "You mean that you're planning to put other kids in there?"

"Of course I am," laughed Trapjaw. "After all, I spent a lot of time designing Spiral Bay."

"What about our parents and the other kids in our class? Aren't they looking for us?"

"I told them that you had been chosen for the interactive math challenge, so they're expecting you home in an hour."

Jack had to do something. He didn't want anyone else getting stuck in Spiral Bay.

He glanced at the clock on the wall and he remembered the words on Trapjaw's note: *The clock is ticking*.

The clock was too high up for Jack to reach, but there was an old crate below it, covered with fishing nets.

**KEY WORDS**

- things
- splutter
- crate
- fishing net

- charge
- leap (leap-leapt-leapt)
- creak
- stretch

- rim
- come loose
- grab

He charged across the room and leapt onto the crate, which creaked under his weight.

"What are you doing?" gasped Becky.

"It's the clock that gives the signal!" said Jack. "If the clock doesn't strike the right hour, the fanfare doesn't sound and the portal can't open."

He stretched up and his fingers met the rim of the clock, pulling and pushing until it came loose from the wall.

"Leave that clock alone," growled Trapjaw, grabbing Jack round the waist.

But it was too late, because even though Jack tried to catch it, the clock flew over his head and fell onto the floor, where a metal shower of springs and cogs burst out of it.

With a loud crack, the crate collapsed and Jack fell to the floor.

A fiery pain shot through his elbow, but it was Trapjaw who let out a shriek like an injured seabird.

Jack, Becky and Arnold left him crouching over the remains of his precious clock, while in the picture behind him, the dark street of Spiral Bay wound down to the inky sea.

**KEY WORDS**

- metal
- shower
- cog
- **burst** (burst-burst-burst)
- crack
- collapse
- fiery
- **shoot** (shoot-shot-shot)
- let out
- crouch
- remains
- inky
- fetch
- embarrassed

Arnold called his parents on his cell phone and asked them
to come and fetch him and his friends.

"We are friends now, aren't we?" he said, looking at Jack and
Becky hopefully.

"Of course we are!" said Becky, giving an embarrassed
Arnold a kiss on the cheek.

"I know one thing," laughed Jack. "Next time we do math,
I'm going to make sure I pay attention!"

# Chapter Five · Comprehension Quiz

**A** Fill in each blank with the right word below.

| begged | gasped | asked | growled |
|---|---|---|---|

❶ "Which one is it?" _______________ Jack.

❷ "Oh, please don't make us go back down to the beach," _______________ Becky.

❸ "That would be 9 p.m.!" _______________ Becky.

❹ "Leave that clock alone," _______________ Trapjaw.

**B** Match the two sides to complete each according to events in the story.

❶ The waves were lapping gently at the shore,  •

❷ They all stood up,  •

❸ Trapjaw stepped forward,  •

❹ With a loud crack,  •

 

• a) a smile on his face.

• b) the crate collapsed and Jack fell to the floor.

• c) washing away Arnold's calculations.

• d) breathing hard in the darkness around the portal.

**C** Choose the best answer to each question.

**❶** Why did Jack tell Arnold to put the numbers in quickly?

    a) He knew that the portal was about to open.

    b) He was hungry and wanted to go home to eat.

    c) He thought that the keypad may not work after dark.

    d) He thought that Arnold might forget the number.

**❷** How did Jack reach the clock?

    a) He knocked it down with a crate.

    b) He asked Becky to get it down for him.

    c) He stood on a crate to reach it.

    d) He stood on his tiptoes until he could reach it.

**D** Put the sentences in order.

**❶** Trapjaw stepped out of the shadows.

**❷** Jack climbed on a crate.

**❸** The children stepped through the portal.

**❹** Jack broke the clock.

    ________ → ________ → ________ → ________

# Let's Review the Story

Fill in the blanks to review the story.

Title: The ______ of the ______

Main Characters: J______, A______, B______, and T______

**Chapter 1**  Setting(s): ______, Jack's ______
Problem: ______'s new ______ is unpleasant.

**Chapter 2**  Setting(s): W______ of O______
Problem: The p______ of S______ B______ changes and comes to l______.

**Chapter 3**  Setting(s): W______ of O______, S______ B______
Problem: J______, B______ and A______ are trapped in S______ B______.

**Chapter 4**  Setting(s): S______ B______
Problem: The children must c______ the G______ R______ to get out of Spiral Bay.

**Chapter 5**  Setting(s): S______ B______, W______ of O______
Problem: The children must calculate when the p______ will o______, and they must stop T______ sending more c______ into S______ B______.
Solution: J______ breaks the c______ that controls the p______.

# Let's Think & Talk

**Think about the following questions and answer them freely.**

❶ The Golden Ratio can be found in many things that we use in our daily lives. Find things around you such as pictures that have the Golden Ratio in them.

❷ Make your own sequence of numbers that has a certain rule. Then, ask your friend what the next number is.

❸ Have you ever found or applied the fundamentals of mathematics that you learned at school in your life? Tell us your experience.

❹ A mathematician is a person who studies and develops math. Besides Fibonacci, what other famous mathematicians do you know? Explain what mathematical theories make them famous.

## Let's Review the Story

Title: The **Secret** of the **Golden Ratio**

Main Characters: **Jack**, **Arnold**, **Becky**, and **Trapjaw**

**Chapter 1**
Setting(s): **school**, Jack's **home**
Problem: **Jack**'s new **teacher** is unpleasant.

**Chapter 2**
Setting(s): **World** of **Oceans**
Problem: The **picture** of **Spiral** **Bay** changes and comes to **life**.

**Chapter 3**
Setting(s): **World** of **Oceans**, **Spiral** **Bay**
Problem: **Jack**, **Becky** and **Arnold** are trapped in **Spiral** **Bay**.

**Chapter 4**
Setting(s): **Spiral** **Bay**
Problem: The children must **calculate** the **Golden** **Ratio** to get out of Spiral Bay.

**Chapter 5**
Setting(s): **Spiral** **Bay**, **World** of **Oceans**
Problem: The children must calculate when the **portal** will **open**, and they must stop **Trapjaw** sending more **children** into **Spiral** **Bay**.
Solution: **Jack** breaks the **clock** that controls the **portal**.

# After-reading Test

- **The Secret of the Golden Ratio**
- **Level 6**
- **26 Questions**

  (Vocabulary 4 / Reading Comprehension 16 /

  Sentence Structure & Grammar 6)

1. What does "genius" mean in the following sentence?

   Becky called Arnold a <u>genius</u>.

   ① someone who is very stupid

   ② someone who is very overweight

   ③ someone who is very greedy

   ④ someone who is very clever

2. What does "delete" mean in the following sentence?

   Becky asked Arnold to <u>delete</u> the number.

   ① erase                    ② change

   ③ improve                  ④ forget

3. What does "reluctantly" mean in the following sentence?

   <u>Reluctantly</u>, Jack allowed himself to be dragged away from the picture and into the lunchroom.

   ① quickly                  ② not wanting to

   ③ with some relief         ④ at last

4. What does "interactive" mean in the following sentence?

   It says there's going to be an <u>interactive</u> math challenge.

   ① being extremely difficult to do

   ② involving people communicating with each other

   ③ having been done before by many people

   ④ frequently occurring late at night

5. Which of the following jobs had Trapjaw NOT done?
   ① magician
   ② actor
   ③ teacher
   ④ game designer

6. Why didn't Jack want to go to "World of Oceans"?
   ① He had been there many times before.
   ② He was scared of fish.
   ③ He felt ill and needed to stay at home.
   ④ He didn't like learning about the sea.

7. Trapjaw said that math was "the key to the universe." What did he mean?
   ① If you understand math, you will rule the universe.
   ② If you understand math, you will know what is beyond the universe.
   ③ If you understand math, you will discover a new universe.
   ④ If you understand math, you will understand how the universe works.

8. How did Arnold spoil the games at recess?
   ① He kicked the ball in the wrong direction.
   ② He kept falling over all the time.
   ③ He told people to do things a different way.
   ④ He pointed at people and laughed at them.

9. Why are golden rectangles often found in art?
    ① They are easy to draw.
    ② They are especially pleasing to look at.
    ③ They represent a secret code.
    ④ They are difficult to paint.

10. Which of these measurements would be correct for a Golden Rectangle?
    ① 10 cm long and 5 cm wide
    ② 12 cm long and 8 cm wide
    ③ 21 cm long and 8 cm wide
    ④ 13 cm long and 8 cm wide

11. Why do you think the author says that Arnold stuck to Jack "like gum on the bottom of his shoe"? Choose two answers.
    ① Arnold wouldn't let go of Jack's leg.
    ② Arnold wouldn't leave Jack alone.
    ③ Jack didn't really want Arnold around.
    ④ Jack was glad that Arnold was with him.

12. Why was Jack looking for the house with yellow curtains?
    ① Becky was in it.
    ② Trapjaw was in it.
    ③ The math challenge was in it.
    ④ The portal was in it.

13. What was strange about the doors on the houses in Spiral Bay?
① They were all rectangular.
② They were unusually tall.
③ They were unusually short.
④ They were all painted green.

14. Why was Becky crying when Jack and Arnold found her?
① She was trapped in the house and couldn't open the door.
② She was upset that Arnold hadn't given her any candy.
③ She was worried that somebody was coming to find her.
④ She was afraid that she would never get out of Spiral Bay.

15. How did the children know that the note was from Trapjaw?
① He had signed his name on it.
② He had told them to look out for his note.
③ He had put his picture on it.
④ He had used the same handwriting as he did at school.

16. Arnold "shook his head and puffed out his cheeks." Why did he do these things?
① He was thinking.
② He was hot.
③ He had a headache.
④ He wanted to scare Becky.

17. Why did Arnold look "thoughtful and almost slightly sad"?
   ① He was missing his parents.
   ② He was worried that he had calculated the ratio incorrectly.
   ③ He liked it in Spiral Bay and wanted to come back.
   ④ He thought that Trapjaw would be disappointed with them.

18. Which sentence is false?
   ① Jack was Becky's brother.
   ② Mom and Dad were searching for them the whole time.
   ③ The portal opened at 9 p.m.
   ④ Trapjaw designed everything in Spiral Bay.

19. Why didn't the portal open every single hour?
   ① It opened randomly.
   ② It opened every second hour.
   ③ It opened according to a pattern.
   ④ It opened during daylight hours only.

20. Why did Jack say that he was going to pay attention the next time they did
   math?
   ① He now thought it was a very interesting subject.
   ② He knew that he was very good at math.
   ③ He wanted to be prepared in case he needed to use math again.
   ④ He thought that Trapjaw was an excellent teacher.

**21.**
> Perhaps it <u>will</u> help <u>us</u> <u>to</u> our task.
>      ①       ②       ③ ④

**22.**
> <u>It</u> was Trapjaw <u>which</u> let out a shriek <u>like</u> an <u>injured</u> seabird.
> ①           ②          ③       ④

※ Choose the correct word or phrase for each blank. (23~25)

**23.**
> He didn't ____________ to think what would happen if he got this wrong.

① even
② barely
③ dare
④ wobble

**24.**
> He said, wriggling about in his seat ____________ he was trying to polish it with his butt.

① though
② as though
③ if
④ even if

25.



① rarely

② slightly

③ doubtfully

④ rather

26. Choose the correct sentence.

① Barely to mention magician, puzzle writer and game designer.

② No to speak magician, puzzle writer and game designer.

③ Not to speak magician, puzzle writer and game designer.

④ Not to mention magician, puzzle writer and game designer.

# Memo 

# Memo

# Memo

Can you solve the
secret of spiral Bay?
The clock is ticking.

**Sarah J. Dodd**

Sarah J. Dodd is an experienced primary school teacher who resides in the UK, but has also taught in Australia. She has a PhD in Science and a certificate in Creative Writing. She has published four books for younger children — 'An Angel Anyway' (Anyway Press) and the Little Angels' series (Lion Hudson plc). Her children's Bible will be published in 2015. She is currently working on a novel for 9-12 year olds and another for young adults.

# The Secret of the Golden Ratio

Written by Sarah J. Dodd
Illustrated by Wanjin Kim

First Published in May 2015

Editorial Manager: Juyon Choi
Editors: Juyon Choi, Hyunjung Kim, Kyunghee Jang, Jiyeong Park
Designers: Eunhee Lee, Elim
Cover Designer: Eunhee Lee

Published and distributed by

Darakwon Bldg., 64-1 Jandari-ro, Mapo-gu, Seoul, Korea 121-894
Tel: 82-2-736-2031(ext. 250)     Fax: 82-2-732-2037
Homepage: www.ihappyhouse.co.kr
Publisher: Kyudo Chung



ISBN: 978-89-6653-193-6 18740 / 978-89-6653-156-1 18740(set)

[Components]
• 1 Audio CD (Recording Studio: Aram)
• Answer Keys & Korean Translation: Free download at www.ihappyhouse.co.kr